I0232583

PORT FOLIO

Sammi Gale is a writer, curator and the editor of Plinth. His poems and short stories have appeared in *Datableed*, *Lighthouse*, *The Toe Rag*, and *The Colorado Review*. His journalism features in *GQ*, *the i Paper*, and *Little White Lies*. He lives in London

© 2025, Sammi Gale All rights reserved; no part of this book may be reproduced by any means without the publisher's permission.

ISBN: 978-1-917617-20-8

The author has asserted their right to be identified as the author of this Work in accordance with the Copyright, Designs and Patents Act 1988

Cover designed by Aaron Kent

Edited and Typeset by Aaron Kent

Broken Sleep Books Ltd
PO BOX 102
Llandysul
SA44 9BG

PRAISE for *Port Folio*

At first *Port Folio* feels like finding the lost pages of Tom Raworth's **Logbook** (it's that good), then it feels like listening to the funniest person you know improvising at gunpoint, derailing every narrative possibility as it emerges while still holding the room. If it stopped for a second to acknowledge the laughter, all would be lost, but on it goes, gleaning and garbling the most absurd gifts of our language environment, building to a kind of besieged intensity that manages (somehow) to be at once alarming, beautiful, hilarious and **totally likeable**.
— Peter Manson

Sammi Gale's blocks of prose poetry track and induce an unblocking, a sensitising of the skin where even cruel impressions glow like hieroglyphs. A child's vivid feel for texture transmutes into an adult's sensual apprehension, whether joyful or painful. A simple act like towelling dry on a beach unfolds whole life cycles from budding to ash, and language brushes the lips.
— John Wilkinson

Gale's business is the transfiguring of language and speech acts. A wine description, an educational tract, economic outlooks, power-lifting, some stern life advice. Here it all becomes prayer-like and incantatory – in that I feel **protected** by poetry when it hits this hard, shielded from received wisdom, secular pieties, ontological cliché, everything that tries to bring us down. *Port Folio* is more life-like than dream-like, but visionary in what it upends and disturbs. Gale's work also has this uneasy and vital engagement with masculinity that I found consoling, provocative and defiant. An artist. This is an enthralling sequence, and I didn't want it to end.
— Luke Kennard

A landlord's unexpected call "chokes a bittercream out my stomach," an unsettled, ambient "churning" that articulates *Port Folio* as intimately and broadly as a voice, a cry that comes from the intestines. Here, in precarious housing that won't hold up, as far from the "jetty" and the "rabbits" as you can imagine, it won't stop. What won't? Answering this question, or being asked it, makes Sammi Gale's poetry, if it's poetry, stun.
— Bhanu Kapil

Port Folio is a bleak breeze — it reconfigures your head in the best possible way.
— Isabel Waidner

CONTENTS

Port Folio

Sammi Gale

Broken Sleep Books

I.

Likely harbour, you passed Sudan wearing a life vest, or it could have been a palmed beach towel. Where touts were a wild blessing I found you rough as a flannel. Hidden, hoping to unfold with humble logic. The bar steward is intimating he's hungry. As you pull the string on your vest, or slip off your bottoms under the towel, you have a flush of sand feeling palatable in the shish bicep gristle I thought was guinea fowl. What's gathering here is a gifted needlepoint defacement where all the saints have arrows sticking out the judgemental parts of their bodies. Your bottoms are now covered in sand that is more parts water than sand. The sunlight could still learn to speak, spell aloud, break even having to sneeze makes my words come thus: I do not even think about it, which you say is pollen. For the past six months perfect record inside where it clots take the vaccine to Dagenham. Cross jockeys will always play lift music, or something like three children shifting to a Greek Zorba. Fine, it starts slow, the first child with a horde of iron filings she's using to fix a cavity, then twenty years later the second child approaches the patriarch of the Zorba and says, 'I want to be vixen.' The patriarch cracks a carbonated drink, the child now an ill-tempered woman from the 1570s, as the dance reaches its late stages, or what appears as a vast and swirling polygonal shape formed by linked hands which we came to call a circle – had the belief been in the first place a burst of colour before your eyes ascribed to swoon of drunkenness – in which the third child, C – through no fault of her own – has become the Zorba's patriarch, giving away left right abandon to the changing velocity of dance, pissing himself in the process, he wishes for a safe blockade where he can wait out the rest of increasing speed, and in the end a dog to finish what's fatigued on the floor. More curious the storm rings out like money against the windows' exterior, and I feel scared guano of cave-dwelling bats who are also at the car wash, and I am twelve, and the brushes and the high-pressure rinse arch are coming to get all of me, rinse me for what worth, and I am gone scared as a spinning brush until someone tells me what I have won. And didn't we wish to eat forget laid waste to youth, and instead this violence wears a fez that is not his to wear it lift it releasing hornets. We talked it over, impossible to stay, how could we afford to feed the lamb and charge our phones overnight and maintain a careful life and work balance. A meaning beyond breath, inescapable as a light filament popping what seemed right. Taking on board more natural fats. The

iron filings will not cement as an impression.
A ding in the bone. We practised in church
between the pews, having been fragments for
a composition that has relevance to your life,
an aria gushed forth from between the gaps in
the staircase opening onto new pay channels
widening to levity compressed now to
industrious bead the potential fed to chickens
in the form of a pellet. O that expenditure or
outflow or detox of feeling the next day brings
with it trust in how the form and structure of
rest must work, as they keep producing pellets,
and a larger and more ecstatic production line
to enforce them. Your wrist for interest. And
your pay gap gallery, sunflower seeds shot
over anyone who needs the distraction, shot
through with rings of ash vitiligo stars are
made of this.

II.

Each departure has the weight and strain of a breadbin. I'm waving on the tundra. Dogs must be carried in case blizzard reality moves you to epidemic rates of affection, shipping forecasts broadcast by modern shepherds, whose caution, by my fair assessment, bled upside into the middle management of their own flocks, all the while acid reflux fluxing more manmade than fiction forever twenty-one with duct tape at the boundaries of the local cricket pitch, watchful for Jill pruning the hedges with change left over for the toilet turnstiles, surprised at having seen shepherds here releasing their early hour bed cast in so much whiteness, Jill's stash reduced fat but at least steel vanishes at freezing point. And yet, as sure as you can spin a bagel at the sun, your face hardening on your tort law textbook what could be got from a shovel saying it bluntly, 'I want to sit on your lap,' even if scalloped for opening your monthly statements, ribbed and all in proportion, at this hour. Obelisks overflowing with ash would fleck shame on you gasping and abandoning hacksaw pitch, beams extending as traffic passes, does a quick stock take, and weeps aloe vera for what the day's gutter ball lashed brilliant, skittish light now distending, and all for moronic ivory! At last.

There are two hands on the bars, spying that which is fled, namely Saint Agatha, still salty from the miso treatment, in the middle of the attic shadow quiet, and the halls of pomade. Resented that the cannons did not dedicate their smoke to me. After the flashes. Or the implicit swan song of boiling rubber. Though I cannot read, and do not know which worldly segment – which hunk, parcel or tranche – would keep, and not discard the guilt lyric, once sent. All I know is polyphenols are components of antioxidant activity, thus desirable. Resented that I did not make manuka honey duty free during the first crescendo of the skin clinics making it rain leaflets right across the road, not giving a harry hazard about the mixed recycling. Though it is true, any the played crumb catches the second lip, dressed the oily of firefighters, the way we all sometimes appear after vespers – much as a boatload of pike was once believed to cure psoriasis. Likely harbour, trapped like a thought forgotten sparrow or passerine flitting in an underground basilica, and isn't Agatha there with a pumice stone touching useless to the char of cannons did not dedicate their days to me. Cold, damp, no-one manning the reception. Unclear where she should put her breasts. Still, switchblade leaflets everywhere, and in the windfall – or (in botanical terms) winged seeds known as samaras – someone is pushing a pram. The pram says, it is easy dying, it is easy to die, only its shutter speed is like a sunken lotus inching its way towards the sand. The life vest is now constricting, more a hindrance than a charm bracelet with charms swinging to the rhythm of a passing train. The passing train is counterfactual; as is the bracelet, the life vest, and state pensions. If the train leaves at 1900 hours, jilting the priest while you blow into the life vest's tube, the pension scheme would only inflate, the charms withering away and helicoptering to ground after a fixed period of time; a time much like dusk; when chihuahuas are scalped in public squares, the business redeems its preference shares. That much was clearly written on that thing you signed but never bothered to read but was all the while available in the prosody itself, loci of rhythmic shock forming a secondary level of meaning available even to marine plankton – even to other dinoflagellates – for crying out. The boom now of chihuahuas echoes through the streets, likely harbour, how big you got while I was away. Nothing more reassuring than touching the artichoke to check it is still there. I figured you were a landmark in the sculpture garden, but not too sculpted, a likeness of a hoodie draped over a bench, spongy tissue scooped out between land and sky.

Our best not to suck, and suckle hope your
zesty hops the landlord calls, chokes a
bittercream out my stomach, really, what
with all this churning of the rudder, etc.,
the butter, the sky, the weather. And it's not
without risk, talking all that Hüsker Dü, and
he would parachute in to speak to the person
in charge, landing in the space after a full
stop. O, my little pickled ambition, likely
harbour, no use panning for golden motes
inside a shaft of light, they're just a metaphor
for a state of mind.

The orangery was scarlet this afternoon.
There were no oranges there. It was late
afternoon. Pits be blind, or glimpsed in
precipitate mesh, I open my eyes, and you
are there, sawing away at a branch, I dread
to think your nine irons put to polishing
Molotov gorgon tosh, by way of the office, no:
an office, now a skittles alley, rain is falling.

With such a recliner saved for a freak and
brief appearance in winter this year backed
by the smell of sage to whisk you away on
public transportation, a bus or a tram, I forget
whose yellow card reader allowed me to touch
in, whose reader was touched by the image
of yellow card, cattle mill all about inside and
swaying so, I was treble. Best not to depart,

only stationary would you place a bet on fauna. Would that I had the paper slip, or a slip of any material, not silk per se.

Passengers were watching, though they said they weren't, as I doused the fire flickering as a shadow in gypsum crystal, a mother staring at her phone's black screen. I crouched to help look under the seats for an earring she'd lost, the fire flickered like a fortune telling, and we stood. I poured the tincture under my tongue. The tincture fell and rolled towards three possible futures. Talk about the trail blazer calling the orangery scarlet. With this idiom, she criticised me for a fault she also possessed.

III.

Rail against the phantoms in the clouds and
get called the city beneath. Squint at the tower
block's glass and get tied to a lamppost as your
owner ducks into a shop. Sniff and skitter the
leaves rebellious and you're a feather suddenly
everyone's an expert witness setting fire to
windmills of feathers held in place by bullet
time cameras as they burn and burn, until
Larkin tells me I'll never learn. But it's hard
to listen when the sound is damp like a cockle
and issuing from a stoma, while respecting the
oldest traditions of wine making in Burgundy.
Our cellar master provides his utmost care to
insure [sic] their perfect maturation. Another
bottle reads thus:

> A kitten nips. And with a Heinz can
> catching drips, once again, that blunt
> edge, Professor Plum, at the hedge,
> with secateurs to take a snap, close
> at hand, a cut will last, a dunnock
> here to reprimand. All day long in
> Sunday best Plum surveys his empty
> nest, tugs the string to plug the gap,
> in wincing sun with bowels in hand go
> to ground now inclined to sneak a nap

It's a pinot noir. There are flames beneath,
frigid, and holding my attention like a pixel.

Soaking in my own discretion. This is inbound marketing, funnel through the leaking cellar and find me. Likely harbour, I want you to find me here, and in this way. Ignite the gaps in my content strategy and scour around for me like a dog with her muzzle in a crisp packet, rip me apart, make me feel like tinsel in the attic, debase me, I have no persona, nor am I search engine optimised, I'm Deliciously Ella uniting simplicity and performance in all weather and all latitudes plus I'm listed right now, Sunseeker, as a toothless Garra rufa fish, nibbling away beneath the Shard, O likely harbour I want to eat the shadow of the bottom of your foot, I will make it into protein shake, I will smoke you through a bassinet.

Prized beyond, wiped down after every use, my hands have never left your sides, a progressive intensity challenge with no perfect record, no sums, only loss of sight so glorious jaundiced by a faint oxidised dream of his mother captured in stained glass, I was yellowing, and so was she. Our family differs from jerky in three distinct ways.

First, the mescaline dries up, pondlike taste in the throat, and there's a bust of Camilla in the entrance hall. Then, with the pond dried and cured, she says there's nothing more boring than relating the dream you had about a poem that started as a receipt and became a yacht, so why put it down. The third future that the tincture rolled into involved metric measurement, a million litres being a megalitre, with my arms open wide, I carried a mirror or I love you this much, with specific gravity of 0.865 relative to pure water, we had been vixens, you were aware of your health, you always bought a newspaper, we sold lemonade in cubic decametres, ever resistant to change, she looked more scared than the Presbyterian church, and you always took an umbrella, just in case.

Likely harbour wasn't made to measure, or blow a fuse, skip or lose a stone or two, be small at first, could call it a phosphate, or the vein of a leaf, but the voice comes from elsewhere, lost as a volume or parcel of air rises. That's after care when the flag goes down you take him inside you, and you are like *The Three Penny Opera* lying supine in a lobster bisque. So that the play of light. To be coupled in the manner of a twin town with a Brancusi fish, so that when one of us is pastoral the other is not pastoral enough, and when one is 'a flashing body seen through water', the other darts away like the reflection of flames in gypsum crystal – but she will say to every harsh sky the colour of roe so ripe with irony it's pollution, 'You are a firmament and not at all the sky you ought to be.' Some other soft sulphate mineral for crying out. The days are getting longer. We cut corners, gill plates, removed the egg skein, only to find our new year's resolutions lay in clusters, while our resolve was fragile membrane carrying round an adagio into the sad traffic and, indicating that the washing was to be performed easy does it, you flicked soap on a thrumming windscreen armed with a smooth rubber blade used to remove or control the flow of liquid on a flat surface. It's cold and hard like a fragment, as silly as a meteorite, when we know very well that a saucepan-full of Listerine spoils the apples, some as big as satellites catch a signal. Good bruiser, protect the estate, sometimes it is easier to read on the train.

Some coral reef or other was bleaching, and the night pastors walked over, handing out exhortations in the form of a lollipops. Lollipops can also be transparent and decentralised. Or limp and obvious like a crown. A pageant be upon those mining towns gone spare, for I want to be used as fertiliser for just now I struck and touched a match to the conifer mean I'm touched that I matched with Jennifer, struck up a casual. She had an average time. Really hamster-wheeling it from the get. You'd better count our cultural and commercial ties when catamarans are being filed down to souvlakia skewers.

Odds are there's a turnstile croaking for all of us, or a postcard folded in four. The feeling that the clouds, reflected in the display window, might be on the edge of someone's seat. The caption 'fields of dust' shimmying in light of the press trip cancelled by his terrific shoes, pitched in minutes is a pain, leave like a fence, for example. The drone of traffic on cloverleaf interchanges shot from above, spaghetti motorways glowing the colour of something preservative, amber, formaldehyde.

IV.

You cough. The sun is a colossal trick based on betting averages that you swallow as a copper coin slips into the pocket. A Tamagotchi kept alive by its place in the sky.

No-one is touching you, escape fruit, sand fly, you canvas tossed with cotton, O galleon rigged with cumin seeds that burn your cheeks to freckles. For the want of sandpaper, backspace these chemtrails are not okay for the square window dragged to the top of a slope submits the forms and leaves the flat the way you found it fermenting in your armpit. Your coattails are a street filled with swags of white flowers marked down for lack of detail, they were ceramic irises and Queen Anne's lace, I promised I would read your palm, but you pulled away. We talked later on the phone.

The blister burst cute ink injected into tapioca, enough to slick your hair back. Even if your background is clouds. CV lists faux-fur as relevant experience. Nine parts perspiration. I don't want you to hear the scraped profiles on a stamp too close to yaw you cheer on a toothache and still it is not the worst warning of thunder that has come this week.

Weathervanes trembling like the aftermath of a jackal. Check your phone. That the palm you scurried inside was raw panicked kitten tongue, the tea flicked by a wind that made everything fade out a song from an era you still stand by. Cruise control, to hope the widget makes a guttural sound like butane, you've muscled out the worried ear, so tell them who designed your wedding cake, in the current climate. Dim light in the mulch underfoot, tunnel down, or it's only you're happy to see me. Diagnostically speaking, your feet leave burning forklike patterns on the pavement, likely harbour, and I rate that a seven. My towel hasn't dried yet.

Cotton shot, once some huge hinge between largo played with dignity now you're all jinxed sparrow phasic and tonic stretch reflexes après ski the colour connects the orange new build with a moorhen. Odds are, as by a jar and takes, but not shingled, dicing the onions so not once reblotted mind the wires are down the rest must waste not wait paste up that freezing poncho.

No-one is like you, then someone leaves when the punch is spiked. The bars flicked by carbs curse taste hash. The whole time I flushed a handful of shells, a centenary on a spiny beach.

Protein cannon dream appears he tongued the town upon approach, touchy links with Stoke while froth builds in the bassinet. But first, traffic speeds, and in it, I filed down a mirror and stoned the empties as an open drunk, lost in the marketplace, I captioned the tap, without pocked life and ground to nitrogenic reds as a Capricorn to greet the sand, thus weather bars to go on without gravity's help, in sun that suspends taste. Flag needs a wash. True north is too famous now to feed us.

He has never stepped towards himself like this. Here, able to do so, through no fault of blue, you fleck glycerol shame hard like the water with next to no effort, litres being megalitres, with my arms open. The display is small art, for the others are swooned. All hail this flavoured orb and a half, with the middle hold and take turns. What we are at twenty clips. Light pollution: 'We ignited it with the UNIFLEX pneumatic cramp inserts and installed even the very heavy or bent fittings so that the return on investment was rapidly achieved. The back wall takes great pride in its lumps and is happy to be cursed – but then, ran on serrated track finding the pulse done in. Timid now, just a copy built in secret. I'll be the bus if customs abort again, whether this or there, it worked, right on track, a grass-fed tomahawk armband, Søren Kierkegaard and Albrecht Dürer tagged each other out, one saved only by the sale of the other. In any case, my mother's life-buoys smoked the phrase taken out, next door go down on Falstaff, go on, go talk at a blood orange. Over at TEFL, I struck out. Even the table flowered. We went inside feeling like a bib spaghettied his back fled that cabled field but I was drowned in The Hague, a dune just in from the backseat folding trays.'

O just to go back a few paces to that big mistake from off the underside of the archway, pinch the tail, gently pull the body out that bespoke chair you are sitting on, hit recline and a business goes broke in Denver. Sift redux in spite the wash sloshing with bootlegged heavens where you belong and yet others where you must grind up nutmeg for courage inside a zeppelin, but that's another Vespa.

I watch one episode, but sleep through the next it makes you devilled eggs and the moon cranks clouds suspended in a dish for weeks until I put the boot through a frozen lake if we are to call our perfume Midnight with a Silver Spoon. I promise to back you always with a pinkie in brine, but the clicker cramping luminol is an unusual brute, and

sends the mailer before I proofed its cheating
cud ebbs instead of paintballs. I need such
trap a basement brisket caps off the night in
stargazing ruin. But as the sun comes up, you
found a publisher for her novel, you host some
data while we get unpacked. Samsung the
psilocybin eight bit tender
if pitch bed ragged its rained on Rizzla
couldn't stuff half the Yale lock through the fork
and jammed up the roads again with greyscale.
A frigate belted on to a plug-in hybrid. An in-
remembrance indoor cactus becomes the most
measured way to speak – ask old Blue Paw.
You've been cropped to fit the waterline and
resized again, but still you won't settle off grid.
The bottom half of you has been Pollocked
across the dashboard, and yet I act like I'm
the one untamed and ready for a sly juice
with breakfast, on the last bramble of which
my skin will clock the Halloween edit should
flat out crease the powder keg hogging the
controller, some of them demanding raises,
while other men want their measurements
and launch bottles, brown 11 oz stubbies and
64 oz growlers, near where we are sitting on
our scratchy beach towels minding our own
Arcadian rhythms and protecting our heads
against the projectiles that are now rocks and
minerals, simple moonstones, towards which,
although I know it annoys you, we can be more

tolerant. One young man breaks away from the group, bringing on gradual wisdom tooth calls for alterations and lights what is in his hand, likely just a pebble, shouts one last time for inseam and outseam and hurls a cricket ball that his father got signed for him by one of the sport's greatest stars, I can see that now it will cut me down. Warm wax in surrounding liquid, I should not be knocked. The two fluids may emulsify, the one surrounding the wax will remain cloudy not clear. This is where my head's at now. You will stand over me on the phone, pacing as the operator asks if you've tried monetising my blog. The sad to ear block's glow next day bod gives what harps on flat in our taped towns finishing with a stop or text chat to win or cheer as the tiles fall off or out to squint into the surf as a mother where this tower block compressed and is now fun to ride in Glico Pocky unmarked cars, books and bingo callers on bank hols in sleeves control flex the hamstrings, ah, but a cheat sheet under the mat, your phone call is in this state of yellow carry on and the wind I can't and not with a face like chewed bottlecaps down it, an example of a lipid and again, up and get it down you stop folding napkins into the wind, the dogs who keep retrieving them and delivering bits of tissue to the owners of Honda Civics need femoral head ostectomies, the

poor dears are down as Dorset Blue Vinney
and the traffic is cosmetic and still it is bad
reception, I can barely hold your hair back.

Cough into here, but before, imagine you are
a cat or snake whose hiss has broken and that
here, where you will hack, is a rag soaked in
chloroform, which occurs naturally in some
types of seaweed. Meanwhile, Penny's sitting
on the M43 going towards a railway station,
thinking of the obscure way she drives, as at
home in fainting as in stucco and the collection
of buttons and dials that were cool to touch.
The loneliest, most accessible prestige credit
card burnt down in its slot, next to the orange
aisle. Enough dying heavy with his fried
Adam's halibut would know. For over a week
the sun set in that velvet tub chair where we
talked for hours, my teeth turned grey from
where I fell on the step and even that will be
passed down like finger food, or I swear I'll
unbox your tongue in the region of the plug.
You sleepwalk through the regular courtesy
call. Insecurities prompt the tantric swing to
get out at me in the night. Rather a small,
tentative thought about costs, about the use of
antiaging mouthwash and you're putting on
all that jawline glide that I can't be certain you
are. Weeks awake in the darkness of those
May moths flittering in condensation while

you have words for the cornflowers and warbles and lizards, the mimosas and melon heads flowered now into a desert of yellow fishes warm and flat like the tea scum I am as I cast her out at last, despite every single one of you saying you wanted me to. I blame the Almighty Peter Butler. I want to be the doctor from the album cover. I would like to scare the Snickers out the vending machine. I put my journal to one side and add to my platform. I host my first video. I scoop the doll house residue into the bowler hat and push that out into the pond and request a detailed description from Plum to make this video a success. I was sleeping because the shade on the ceiling, because the moonlight on the gauze saw that I was awake, and I crept into the path of a dog or a cat and he or she rushed in a blur, well, the tap's not dripping anymore and we still have our guidebook, our Mary Janes leading back to the bridge, only that last mile even if it is fake will leave us in a ditch uproot the conifers I mean matched with Jennifer drifts at 'bagging / his dome the first one to stop lagging' erstwhile links to a far-off bedrock fracture clung to you like a single hair you place a bid, get engaged, but I am here mainly to promote my poem by turning it into Emsculpt, to deliver the equivalent of one thousand ethically disposed of lithium-ion batteries. With Lily and Georgina asleep by the time you receive this little update, I'll make sure you do not pay any tax on strawberry soda or polyurethane furniture with Krispy core insulation, and I'll be paid in leeks to end your adventures in the country. Make a paste of myself and dance to whatever you are singing, I know I'll have their vote. O autoerotic lock on the door, can't we pipe some sound in! Today the sun is bright, it rages through our fingers and the sand is soft and the boatman is fishing his partner out the river, and if it was our boat it could stomach two-thirds of my account and he is yelling up the river from the lake, still swimming it up as I hit my head on the corner of the island, but I don't know who you are and the sea is so blue, while every hole I shoot through has sea in it, the girl at Waco said so. The rain is so light, it falls to pieces and my head tells me it is not rain but crystalline silica dust and my food bank is selling Christmas wrapping paper that follows you to the door as strong as a power cable made for sitting through long days in the chair in the sun, some exercise before our game of twosome getting it down me with two hundred perch and you donning something like a belted blouse with sleeves and ease of movement and the vapours passing through. We go for the cheeseburger

that once looked like a bird and was formed of
a sea of bits of cinephiles all facing the table, a
hundred micrograms in a breath, at least high
rates in the news with the drop in vendors
means a government that lacks the funds for
doing the equivalent of sitting on a knife, and
as a journalist the bipolar storm chaser has
your hand in making knots on the floor and
puts you on speaker and makes use of the
antidepressants clustered in the bathroom
drawer, while the body near a bus stop tasered
on this site of enduring stupidity like
divebombing tubular bells that have been
enshrined into our concept of a 'wall', so how
often, you ask, should a twenty-three-year-old
pull a person who just got into a car out of the
seat while yanking his seatbelt on, and how,
when a plane flips and all of its oxygen masks
deploy, do we decide which bathroom to
decorate first, you are right, you will let me
stay as long as I like but no longer than first
half I hope I'll see you all there, to break from
the static that's being fought by all the people
above 14,000 feet you find yourself tying a
clove hitch and then a taut-line hitch to
maintain tension, plus they've got the vast,
high-powered fans humming through their
beards and hats to keep the gloaming off their
ears, but what you *can* blame them for is the
way the harvesters work: crawl through that

buffer blasted soup while you rub your beak in my skull, the windows cleaned once a day, a bunch of new teams come in to trim the clotheslines and fit the jets in my roof to keep the bugs out since I'm only a featherweight, the salt of our licked envelopes can't tell the people around us who is living, and my fear is that I will get blocked and we'll just float there, in a mixture of flesh, battered mice, paper clips, carbon, and our lives, our mirrors, our razors – or am I just being a Pablo at the post office for thinking this? Left all the memory foam at the front of the room, maybe to look at the open door as well. When I visited, the telephone was being used to speckle and spot towns and buildings like a stealthy brush of snow on the pavements of dirty cathedrals. Did they make any money for the city? We've all done it. Who among us carrying the furniture, pinched and radiating outwards. The context. It is a recession. Perhaps he'll bring her home and sit in his armchair, above the Great Wall, while the traffic rotates above the dome like freezer burn, as if waiting to merge. One is torn between hope that it'll fit and the desire to swerve off to a corner and unplug it. Inside a curve. Fresh paint. Watching cough syrup in plastic is a pink diffusing mist. I'm already tired of pink like a typo in these translucent skins of palm trees and red as the brown lights of Las Vegas, powdered. The actual opening is covered with black plastic which billows in the wind. This is the first time I've seen the anti-sky of Dublin, the clouds like bad guitar solos, a couple break open, and there's an ice cream van here on the bay. 'Make me a sundae, please', reads the note from his sister in an envelope addressed to Kennedy. Just now at headache desk stranded on the sixth floor, I have one in my bag, another inside a mouth, three more lost in the door handle, a few in the floor, a couple engaged at the sink, while on the back bench beside the cup of hot water, so near, so cold, like one of those homicidal mummies you see in the Alps in winter, face down with its wig scraping the ground, he reschedules the conference and everything in between. Losing your head over the under-cooked pizza, and the postman hasn't been to work for ten days, he's just a part of the city in a sugary plumage, a note that it's actually more like six weeks, a stone that turns a log of wood into an irrelevant problem, an egg timer, an optional electrical back up for our hearts but not our heads, 'floating' with joy in the pores of your father's skin, a feeling not reciprocated, like a bit part in my friend's play, and when I finally tell you my parents' names, your feet don't know whether they are on or off. On 12 September

2017, my housemate will die and my bookshelf will be lonely. Let's eat. Then I'll tell you. But to be running non-stop would destroy the family album, which is why my poem, as well as being a landscape, is a kind of sickness you'll have to take off your shoes to see, though. Shaking with anger in front of the artichokes. The tour starts on the left, and as the wormhole arches through the sky, the grey clouds fall away, past the grandparents, nieces and nephews, but also through their reflections in the hill behind the stables, in my head, or on the iPad, they are like the places where we used to live, but also how the horses, which used to be at the gate, where you would run, past them, the clouds falling, I remember that, so when they are gone, just think, the clouds were still there, but all the horses were gone, all you could see were horses and a bevy of larks, those Walkabouts and All Bar Ones sound all the better to date you with unlimited skips, you're waiting for the rain, but the clouds are empty, but your face is there, in the shadows, falling and raining, and it sounds you could be a pickled peach testing the hug, bounce and firmness of the mattress. My housemate's mother is not coping well. Listening to Anon and Amanda Palmer on the deck of a ship during a storm, likely harbour, the language she writes in, the people who beat us when the fog pulls the living up from sleep and deposits them on the lower floors of hospitals, that is, on the pavement and then carries them away. For this type of work, I would have to get comfortable looking death in the dumplings that break like pearls, cassoulet that spills into your mouth, walking into rooms while you're on fire. The blacksmiths in Reykjavik and little boys in Sierra Leone blow hard at tire rings. But do let us know when the track is over. I will check the expiry dates on all the plastic bottles on the whole aisle to see how long we have left, but it sounds forced to read from a teleprompter, so goes the hype. I'm back in the office on Tuesday morning, on the phone to New York, booking tickets to the opening of Once in a Blue Moon in June. I'm talking to my wife about what I would like to do with her with the aid of a harmonium and a thousand little ring binders turn into shrapnel as they circle above and then a little more and the light is a candle in this little, I guess, 'room' but I can't be sure because I'm talking to my wife about house prices and Sotheby's, an increasingly unstable climate, and I'm wondering about adjusting my future novel's opening to include a region devastated by war and freak weather events. You open your coat, or your shirt, or your, you know, it has a pattern, it is fringed with light that gets livelier when you rub the towel over your skin, and I know I can't say. I'm waiting for the departure announcement for the flight to San Francisco to see my partner and her new baby. We've booked an Airbnb and plan to see Yosemite. When we reach the valley, a family is to the right of us, and of course, it will take me months to look over all these paragraphs, check every frog's vocal sac, get into the otters and eels of it, the Craigslist denim. Please be advised that your mother's friend, the florist, would like to believe she really means well. What kind of thread-the-needle spends the best part of his life carrying bricks to the hole in the wall where his liver should be just to shift shadows that fade to green available for download for a snip at £9.99, or as a Kindle eBook for £5, or as squid ink looking to get in to a hostel for the night, but without the latest Lifestyle News. Next, we chase a fox across the hills. Burnt lumps of undelivered dildos. They're probably the same in Beijing. Going down the stairs, I do remember some of the good times, see the dim shape of my mother smiling at me. From now on the square mile will be however far you get with these trolleys and Go-Pros. Gulp of my own grief before the midday meal. We'll wait for the lake to cool to drinking temperature, then close our eyes, knowing that in the night, even in our nightmares, we can smooth out the transitions like the skulls of parakeets and this is a fibreoptic hangnail for the hum of her rock of Gibraltar shockproof as a leap year, some were already on to lunch at the next venue, some hadn't seen his shearling, and there is dust on my fingers but I wipe my hand slides down the sharp edge and I make a little cloud, the cloud rises into my mouth, tastes like beans and freezer burn, and I just feel this heat like I'm a leafcutter ant with a leaf, I won't discuss it further, even though I think this might be the final clause for me, everything is so fenced in now, the sextet has become a quartet, that's four if you count the superimposed floor-plan, which contains a woman's flat, the floors all the same, about to be peeled off one by one, to reveal the Astroturf, likely harbour, I know, the only thought that could settle me down is I wish you would just fucking subscribe. When I was a child, you would bring back rabbits and mice from the hills. When we get to the jetty, which is the moon, on the beach you hear me cry I feel like it's the wetsuit that is too tight, a tear in the map that is empty of lakes that we drank. The beds, when they were made for us, were white. These days I'm sleeping on the fold-out air conditioning system, which has black mould on the drawers and is very tall and skinny and quiet and has a door that you can shut when you're tired, and if anyone would like to stand behind the door and say something rude to me, I wouldn't hear it through the raised panels that barely stand, it's hardly the tuning fork that kept us dancing on the edge of safety, under the jackboot of power reference the homeless peel off down a street on a bike and I don't know whether to call the police or watch them smash into a nearby house and become Special K saplings and spring through your throat, as mentioned, he can find the road out, trust me he's bugged very easily by punching a hole in the side of the can, near the bottom, placing his mouth over the hole, and pulling the tab to open the top an X-ray sing this sunbeam sadness that's clogged up in my face, please leave me alone for a minute, I am thrilled and thrashing to bits like a dairymaid sent over on a motorbike or a bullfighter from the kit who cuts through the long grass going to the seaside where the first chap called Serapio who 'wants to see the ocean' will perhaps shout at him, the poor pupfish, there'll be one in the tank one to keep a lookout at the cash-in, but if it does not fly over the English Channel kick back with claggy Diesel fumes as it passes through a door with uncertain curtains and cutlery in it, then you still stick to its concave chest during a derby picked by chance by an employee-finding tool gives you complete access to upwards of six modems on your end before they hit Joe Public and onwards, you complete waste of Valium and goose down in your pilfered life vest, you made it through clearing only to tape my own death with a moving reference to Napoleon and £50 off if you recommend me to a friend. The way you turn a tantrum into a coffee-table book that I am holding up in triumph, in every way, ad nauseam, multi-level, how to use it in a sentence, our most recent beta-testing phase demanded we let it pass as the rook flies, upon highness in the cucked way I say 'hieroglyphs' as I lift my arm and pour more Oxo into the fishing rods lost in play. Marry your dead. Go to their funeral. Pick up their ashes. Get dropped by your label. Go home, prescription breeze in the soul. They're fucking dead.

V.

Going to the gym is like buying wholesale in a stanza, so I punched through the wall: a multicoloured hummingbird with a thermal core frazzling the daylight savings out the sector preparing to glue itself to public space wearing a metal cowl, strip lighting, flower beds and antique fishing flies 'from the early 1900s, the majority made in South Africa' hosts a pity party for that fig leaf based on Alastair Treadwell, he's the one who spiked that volleyball akimbo. Below deck we are the pilot light grade eight clingfilmed the cat to the grotto, barely news, likely harbour, they will never get me out your gross swaddling an empty burger bun in the gumshoe of the marquee, unaware the net curtain stuck to the sole of my shoe like a cape. Munch. A binman throws his chain into the night and it rattles. I would rather throw the other Royal Holloway vampy bones, teeth, the lone toenail that marks the bad sex we had in the attic with the insulation. 'You don't have a pension, do you?' says the waitress, as if she could sit inside a photobooth for years till it began to grow a bubble and we could pop it with a needle. Perhaps they don't have arts degrees? Nothing in this green piece of kerplunk can match what is on tonight. You run in socks on warm stones and this makes it fly like chunks of a Stone Age axe.

I pour his ashes over my garden, sip my third cup in the library chair facing you, likely harbour. Two hands on the tiller. Wailing into wan trees. Blistered lips as the sun flares away on a tiny stool by the garage window, and the opening notes cut the burdock heads off into likely harbour, milk the swallowtail for one last dance on the high floor, one between heat waves and radiator blinks us petals in the air, a second on the lips, a lifetime with you in the waves and waves of bleary traffic.

ACKNOWLEDGEMENTS

Thanks always to Emily, my partner in all things. Thanks to Mae for reading early drafts. To Aaron and Broken Sleep Books for giving this poem a home. To George, Jeremy, and Keston, for helping shape the way I write. And to that unfinished novel that almost finished me — thanks for the margins.

LAY OUT YOUR UNREST

www.ingramcontent.com/pod-product-compliance
Lightning Source LLC
LaVergne TN
LVHW041311080426
835510LV00009B/949